Dolmat Alla Vladimirovna

Chthonic twenty-four hours in literature

Dolmat Alla Vladimirovna

Chthonic twenty-four hours in literature

ScienciaScripts

Imprint

Any brand names and product names mentioned in this book are subject to trademark, brand or patent protection and are trademarks or registered trademarks of their respective holders. The use of brand names, product names, common names, trade names, product descriptions etc. even without a particular marking in this work is in no way to be construed to mean that such names may be regarded as unrestricted in respect of trademark and brand protection legislation and could thus be used by anyone.

Cover image: www.ingimage.com

This book is a translation from the original published under ISBN 978-620-2-06660-0.

Publisher:
Sciencia Scripts
is a trademark of
Dodo Books Indian Ocean Ltd. and OmniScriptum S.R.L publishing group

120 High Road, East Finchley, London, N2 9ED, United Kingdom
Str. Armeneasca 28/1, office 1, Chisinau MD-2012, Republic of Moldova, Europe
Printed at: see last page
ISBN: 978-620-7-91353-4

Table of contents

Introduction

Truly great is the man who manages to master his time. Hesiod There is a sullen night on the vault of the slumbering heavens; In silent stillness the dell and the groves are silent, In gray mist the distant forest is silent; The brook, running into the shade of the oak-tree, is slightly heard, The breeze, asleep on the leaves, is slightly breathing, And the silent moon, like a majestic swan, Floats in the silvery clouds.

It floats, and with its poor rays it illuminates the objects around it.

A.S. Pushkin

Literature and time... These two concepts sometimes accommodate fantastic things - the literary chronotope and the unreal world. In the end, we will talk about chthonic twenty-four hours in literary monuments and in the lives of the torchbearers of works - poets and writers. Chthonic twenty-four hours place the heroes of works in the sphere of forces and values, from which only deeds can be born.

The purpose of our research work was as follows: to investigate the significance of chthonic twenty-four hours in the literature.

The objectives were:

1. Examine the structure of the day

2. Find the etymology of the chthonic twenty-four hours

3. Analyze literary chronotope using examples of irreal images in literature

4. Identify the difference between real-time and irreal-time literary characters

5. To show the influence of chthonic twenty-four hours on the work and life of writers 6. Systematize the results obtained.

While investigating this concept, a hypothesis was put forward: how do chthonic twenty-four hours influence the disclosure of literary images and the creation of writers. The objects of the research were literary works with irreality and some life facts of writers.

The following methods were used in the study:

1. Study of popular science literature

2. Comparative analysis

3. Compilation of eidos outlines to reveal the concept of chthonic twenty-four hours

4. Questionnaire survey on the problem.

The works of F. Dostoevsky "White Nights" and "Crime and Punishment", A. S. Pushkin "Eugene Onegin", "The Prophet", L. N. Tolstoy "War and Peace", M. N. Bulgakov "The Master and Margarita", N. V. Gogol "Viy" and "Evenings on a Farm near Dikanka", V. V. Shakespeare "Hamlet" were studied.Bulgakov "The Master and Margarita", N.V. Gogol's "Viy" and "Evenings on a Farm near Dikanka", V. Shakespeare's "Hamlet", V.A. Zhukovsky's "Svetlana", S. Esenin's "Black Man", J.V. Goethe's "The Forest King". This choice is not accidental. For example, Dostoevsky's heroes from "White Nights" lead an active life under the cover of the moon, and Raskolnikov sees the madness of this world when he is unconscious.

A general idea of the twenty-four hours

A day (plural of the ancient form clash, junction meaning "the junction of day and night") is a unit of time measurement, approximately equal to the period of the Earth's revolution around its axis.

A day usually refers to the astronomical concept of a solar day. In common usage, a day is often called a day.

A day is divided into 24 hours (1440 minutes, or 86400 seconds) and consists of day, evening, night, and morning.

Calendar days make up weeks, months.

A day in astronomy

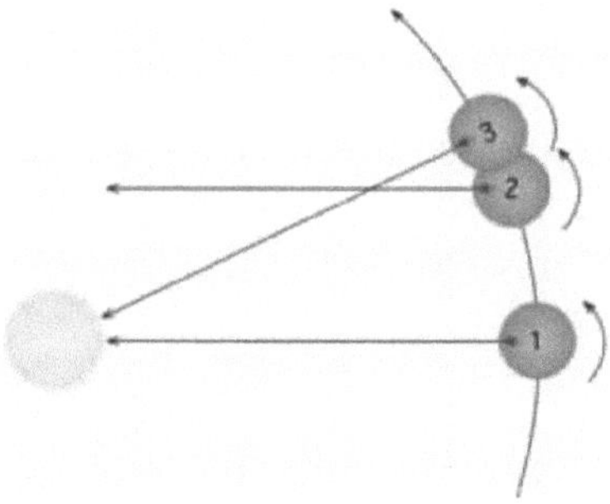

Comparison of the duration of stellar (2) and solar (3) days at coincidence of orbital and proper rotation directions

This is the time interval between the two upper culminations of the luminary - true noon. The duration of the day on a planet depends only on the angular velocity of its own rotation. If a distant star is chosen as the luminary, then, unlike the central luminary of the planetary system, such a day will have a different duration. For example, on Earth we distinguish between an average solar day (24 hours) and a stellar day (23 hours 56 minutes 4 seconds). They are not equal to each other because, due to the Earth's orbital motion around the Sun, for an observer located on the Earth's surface, the Sun shifts against the background of distant stars.

The average solar day is tied to a fictitious "average Sun" - a point moving uniformly along the equator, making one revolution in one year. The real Sun moves unevenly along the ecliptic due to the ellipticity of the Earth's orbit, then lagging behind the average Sun in longitude, then ahead of it, so the true solar day (the time between the two true noon) varies in duration during the year.

The value of a day is not included in the SI, but it can be used in calculations. In this case 1 day is taken to be exactly 86,400 seconds. In astronomy, a day defined in this way in SI seconds is called a Julian day.

The mean solar day, however, does not contain an integer number of seconds (for example, its duration at epoch 2000.0 was 86400.002 s), and the duration of the mean solar day is also variable due to the secular variation of the angular velocity of the Earth's rotation. In this connection, it is periodically necessary to bring the UTC atomic <u>Universal Coordinated Time</u> in accordance with the <u>UT1 mean solar time</u> (based on the Earth's rotation). In this case, a pre-announced <u>coordination second</u> ("leap second") is added or subtracted to the day on <u>June 30</u> or <u>December 31.</u>

In SI, a second is defined as 9,192,631,770 periods of radiation corresponding to a transition between two <u>superfine</u> levels of the ground state of the <u>cesium-133</u> atom. Based on this definition, a strict definition of a day would be 794,243,384,928,000 such transitions.

In other languages

As mentioned above, the term "*day" is* often replaced by the word "day", but in any case, the Russian language has words to unambiguously separate the concepts of "day" (daylight hours) and "day" (24 hours). A separate word for "day" also occurs in the following languages: .

Hebrew *PtiW-* yemama;

- Swedish *dygn*;

- Dutch *etmaal*

- Belarusian *sutkg* (similar to Russian);

- Ukrainian *doôà*;

- Polish *doba*;

- Lithuanian;

- Latvian *diena*;

- Bashkir *teulek*.

In <u>English, a</u> *day is* usually denoted by the word day, which has the basic meaning of "day". When it is necessary to designate a day, the term "24 hours" or "day and night" is used. There is also a special term <u>nychthemeron </u>(from <u>Greek </u>night and day), but this term will not be understood by everyone. For the word "twenty-four hours" in English the term "twenty-four to seven" or "24/7" is used, which literally means "24 hours, seven days a week".

This is similar in most other languages that do not have a separate word for day.

The concept of chronotope

To keep track of time, a chronometer is used: for example, an <u>alarm clock</u>. **Time is** one of the basic concepts of <u>philosophy</u> and <u>physics, a</u> conventional comparative <u>measure of the motion of matter, as</u> well as one of the coordinates of <u>space-time,</u> along which the <u>world lines of physical bodies</u> are stretched.

In <u>philosophy, it</u> is an <u>irreversible</u> flow (flowing only in one direction - from the <u>past,</u> through the <u>present</u> to the <u>future)</u>[III] , within which all the <u>processes</u> existing in <u>being, which</u> are <u>facts,</u> take place.

In the quantitative (metrological) sense, the concept of **time** has three aspects:

- coordinates of the event on the <u>time axis</u>. In practice, it is the current time: calendar time, defined by <u>calendar</u> rules, and <u>time of day,</u> defined by some time numbering system (scale) (examples: <u>local time, Coordinated Universal Time</u>);

- relative time, the time interval between two events;

- subjective parameter when comparing several <u>different frequency</u> processes.

Properties of time

First of all, time is characterized by its directionality (see "<u>Arrow of time</u>"). Also, time is defined in some reference <u>frame,</u> which can be either *non-uniform* (the process of the Earth's rotation around the Sun or the human pulse) or *uniform*. The uniform reference frame is chosen "by definition", earlier, for example, it was associated with the motion of bodies of the solar system (<u>ephemeris time</u>), and nowadays it is locally considered to be <u>atomic time,</u> and the <u>standard of a second</u> is 9,192,631,770 periods of radiation corresponding to the transition between two <u>superfine levels of the</u> ground state of <u>caesium-133</u> atom in the absence of perturbation by external <u>fields.</u> It should be noted that this definition is not arbitrary, but is related to the most accurate periodic processes available to mankind at this stage of development of experimental physics[121] .

Most modern scientists believe that the distinction between the past and the future is **fundamental**. According to the current level of scientific development, <u>information is</u> transferred from the past to the future, but not vice versa. The <u>second beginning of</u> <u>thermodynamics</u> also points to the accumulation of <u>entropy in the</u> future.

However, some scientists think a little differently. <u>Stephen Hawking</u> in his book "A <u>Brief</u> <u>History of Time: From the Big Bang to Black Holes</u>" disputes the claim that for physical laws there is a distinction between the direction "forward" and "backward" in time. Hawking justifies this by arguing that information transfer is only possible in the same direction in time in which the total entropy of the <u>universe</u> increases. Thus, the <u>Second Law of</u> <u>Thermodynamics</u> is trivial because entropy grows with time because we measure time in the direction in which entropy grows[121].

The singularity of the past is considered highly plausible. The opinions of scientists regarding the presence or absence of various "alternative" versions of the future vary[141].

Time dependence

Since the states of our world depend on time, the state of any system can also depend on time, as it usually happens. However, in some exceptional cases, the time dependence of a quantity may be negligibly weak, so that this characteristic can be considered to be independent of time with high accuracy. If such quantities describe the dynamics of any system, they are called **conserved quantities**, or **integrals of motion**. For example, in <u>classical mechanics,</u> the total energy, total momentum, and total momentum of an isolated system are integrals of motion.

Various physical phenomena can be categorized into three groups:

. **stationary** - phenomena whose main characteristics do not change with time. The <u>phase</u> <u>portrait of</u> a stationary phenomenon is described by a fixed point;

. **nonstationary** - phenomena for which the time dependence is essentially important. The phase portrait of a nonstationary phenomenon is described by a point moving along some trajectory. They, in turn, are divided into:

. **periodic** - if there is a clear periodicity in the phenomenon (phase portrait - closed curve);

- **quasi-periodic** - if they are not periodic in the strict sense, but on a small scale look like periodic (phase portrait - almost closed curve);

- **chaotic** - aperiodic phenomena (phase portrait - an unclosed curve that covers some area more or less uniformly, an attractor);

- quasi-stationary - phenomena which, strictly speaking, are nonstationary, but the characteristic scale of their evolution is much larger than the times of interest in the problem.

There is currently no single universally recognized theory explaining and describing such a concept as Time. There are many theories (they can also be part of more general theories and philosophical teachings) trying to justify and describe this phenomenon.

In classical physics, time is a continuous quantity, an a priori characteristic of the world, which is not defined by anything. As a basis of measurement, a certain, usually periodic, sequence of events is used, which is recognized as a standard of some time interval. This is the basis for the principle of clock operation.

Time in classical physics exists by itself, separate from space and any material objects in the world. Time, as a flow of duration, equally determines the course of all processes in the world. All processes in the world, regardless of their complexity, have no influence on the course of time. Therefore, time in classical physics is called absolute. I. Newton: "Absolute, true mathematical time by itself and by its very essence, without any relation to anything external, runs uniformly, and otherwise called duration .... All movements can be accelerated or decelerated, but the course of absolute time cannot change." The absoluteness of time is mathematically expressed in the invariance of the equations of Newtonian mechanics with respect to Galileo's transformations. All moments of time in the past, present and future are equal to each other, time is homogeneous. The flow of time everywhere and anywhere in the world is the same and cannot change. To each real number can be put in correspondence to a moment of time, and, vice versa, to each moment of time can be put in correspondence to a real number. Thus, time forms a continuum. Similar to the arithmetization (matching each point to a number) of points in Euclidean space, one can arithmetize all points of time from the present indefinitely backward into the past and indefinitely forward into the future. Only one number is needed to measure time, that is, time is one-dimensional. Intervals of time can be corresponded to parallel vectors, which can be added and subtracted as line segments. The most important consequence of the homogeneity of time is the law of conservation of energy.

The equations of <u>Newton's mechanics</u> and <u>Maxwell's electrodynamics</u> do not change their form when the sign of time is reversed. They are symmetric with respect to time reversal (<u>T-symmetry</u>). Time in <u>classical mechanics</u> and <u>electrodynamics is</u> reversible.

The origin of the chthonic twenty-four hours

Khthonic DEMONS - (from Greek khthonios - underground), various creatures appearing in myths, such as ancient Greek harpies and erinyes, Indian rakshasas, Arabian djinns, Germanic elves and Valkyries, and the like. They are symbols of thanatic forces associated with death in various guises.

Chthonic beings (from Greek khthonios - underground), mythological characters and animals associated with the underworld and with the productive power of the earth (water). In the Slavic tradition, chthonic creatures were primarily creepers, which included animals associated with death and the netherworld, including the raven, wolf and others. To the chthonic creatures belonged, according to the reconstructed Slavic myths, serpent-like opponent of the thunderer. In Slavic tradition, many domestic animals - goat, horse, etc. - were endowed with dual nature; their ritualized death (sacrifice) was supposed to contribute to the fertility of the earth and so on.

CHTHONIC - (from Greek khthonios - subterranean), belonging to the gods and spirits of the underworld. (Big Dictionary of Esoteric Terms)

Chthonic deities (from Greek χθων, "earth, soil") - in many religions and mythologies - deities that originally personified the forces of the underworld, i.e. the world under the earthly (human world) universe and under the heavenly (air, clouds) beginning - the "underworld". Representatives in the animal world are various "creepers" (reptiles), fish, "harmful" insects, and in some cases birds (crows, magpies, sparrows, etc.).

Later, chthonic deities became an integral part of pantheistic religions, sometimes occupying a predominant position in them (until they were supplanted by the cults of celestial and solar deities).

Chthonic beings also included deceased ancestors living in the afterlife (underworld). Chthonic character is also characterized by the rivals of the demiurge - the lords of the underworld.

Chthonic twenty-four hours is a time of unreality that expands the 24 hours.

It is a different co-dimension, a space that opens up what cannot be seen or comprehended in real life.

Chthonic twenty-four hours are the result of unspent energy and potential, which does not allow a person to calm down, brings his nervous system into a state of excitement and makes him create.

The concept of chronotope in literary statements

Man is **amazingly** human - he is grieved when he loses wealth, and indifferent to the fact that the days of his life are irrevocably gone.

Abu'l-Faraj

Minutes are long and years are fleeting.

A. Amiel **Time** is the capital of the mental worker.

O. Balzac

In the important affairs of life one must always hurry as if the loss of a single minute should have caused everything to perish.

B. G. Belinsky

Time is a great teacher, but unfortunately it kills its students.

Г. Berlioz **Time is a** great teacher.

Э. Burke To **choose** time is to save time, and what is done untimely is done in vain.

Ф. Bacon **Time** is the greatest of innovators.

Ф. Bacon **One** of the most irretrievable losses is the loss of time.

Ж. Buffon

He who does not know the value of time is not born to glory.

Л. Vovenargue You can expect everything from time and people.

Л. Wovenarg

It only takes one minute to be amazed, it takes years to do an amazing thing.

К. Helvetius

The two greatest tyrants on earth: chance and time.

И. Herder

Truly great is the man who manages to master his time.

Hesiod

Order teaches you how to save time.

И. Goethe You can **always** find enough time if you use it well.

И. Goethe

The loss of time is hardest on the one who knows the most.   *И. Goethe*

Times change, and we change with them.   *Horace*

What the all-destroying time does not weaken.   *Horace*

All that is hidden now will be revealed in time.   *Horace*

A person who chooses to waste even one hour of his time has not yet grown to realize the full value of life.

Darwin

No matter **how** fast time flies, it moves extremely slowly for someone who only observes its movement.

C. Johnson

The significance of the chthonic twenty-four hours in literary works and the lives of writers

A symbol, breathing millennia, sinister chthonika, the lust of death, the stench of its power.... Only a cosmonaut, who in his daily life is constantly confronted with chthonika, observing the every-second penetration of chaos into our world, will be able to absorb the monsters without a shudder, sending them into the irretrievable abyss of his cruel deconstructing womb. Literary creators can also be called a kind of cosmonauts.

Tatiana, the heroine of Pushkin, like Svetlana of Zhukovsky, learns the future through fortune-telling, coming into contact with the otherworld.

Here is how Pushkin characterizes Tatiana Larina in the novel "Eugene Onegin" at the moment of prophetic dreaming

XXIII

What was the consequence of the date?

Alas, not hard to guess!

Love's maddening misery

They haven't stopped worrying

A young soul, a sadness greedy;

No, more than a sad, sad passion

Poor Tatiana's on fire;

Her bed sleep runs;

Health, life's color and sweetness,

A smile, a pristine peace,

Gone is all the sound of nothing,

And sweet Tanya's youth fades:

That's how the storm's shadow wears

A day barely born.

The quote "Barely a day is born" suggests that our heroine is entering a state of chthonic twenty-four hours.

The image of the young poet Vladimir Lensky is permeated with chthonic images. One gets the impression that this hero constantly resides in other worlds. The following chapters from the text serve as confirmation

VI

To my village at the same time

A new landlord has arrived

And equally rigorous scrutiny

In the neighborhood, the occasion was served:

By the name of Vladimir Lensky,

With a soul straight from Göttingen, A handsome man in full bloom, Kant's admirer and poet.

X

He sang love, love obedient,

And his song was clear,

Like the thoughts of a simple-minded maiden, Like a child's dream, Like the moon In the deserts of the serene sky, Goddess of mysteries and tender sighs. He sang of separation and sorrow, And something, and misty distance, And romantic roses;

He sang those distant lands, Where long into the bosom of silence his living tears poured; He sang the faded color of life At not a little eighteen years old.

If we examine the text of the novel, it is safe to say that in this work A.C. Pushkin leads two worlds in parallel: chthonic and real. Let us read:

XIII

My friends, what's the use?

Maybe it was heaven's will,

I'll stop being a poet,

I'll be possessed by a new demon,

XIX

My goddesses! What are you? Where are you?

Hear my sad voice:

Are you still the same? Different maidens,

By replacing you, they didn't replace you?

And in defiance of Thebes' threats,

I will humble myself to humble prose;

An old-fashioned romance novel, then.

Will take up my cheerful sunset.

Not the agony of secret villainy

I will portray it menacingly,

But I'm just gonna tell you

The legends of the Russian family,

Love's captivating dreams

The mores of our old days.

Will I hear your choruses again?

Will I behold the Russian Terpsichore

A soul-filled flight?

Or the dull eye will not find

Familiar faces on a boring stage,

And, staring into the alien light.

Disappointed lorgnette,

The spectator is indifferent to the fun,

I'll yawn silently

And reminisce about the past?

A.S. Pushkin writes about the existence of chthonic twenty-four hours and irreal predictions and meetings in the poem "The Prophet"

And the six-winged seraphim appeared to me at the crossroads;

V.A. Zhukovsky can be said to be an entirely chthonic poet. In fact, any of his works is connected with chthonic creatures, and the action takes place, for the most part, during the chthonic twenty-four hours. Literally from the first lines he places his Svetlana in an unreal world, which later affects the heroine's life in reality.

Once a baptismal evening

The girls were guessing:

Outside the gate is a slipper,

Off his foot, thrown;

The snow was being shoveled; under the window

Listened to; fed

Counting chicken with grain;

The fierce wax was being drowned;

He sits down in front of the mirror;

She was secretly shy

Looking in the mirror;

It's dark in the mirror; all around

Dead silence;

A candle with a flickering flame

A little glow pours down....

The timidity in her stirred her breast,

She's afraid to look back,

In a bowl of pure water

They put a gold ring on it,

The earrings are emerald;

They spread out a white board

And over the bowl they sang in harmony

The songs are subluded.

The moon shines dimly

In the gloom of the fog

Silent and sad

Sweet Svetlana.

Here's a pretty one;

Fear fogs the eyes...

With a crackle, a light flickered,

A cricket shrieked pitifully,

Midnight Herald.

propped up on your elbow,

A little bit of Svetlana's breathing...

Here. easy lock

Someone knocked, he heard it;

Shyly looking in the mirror:

Behind her shoulders.

Someone seemed to be shining

With bright eyes...

The chthonic twenty-four hours are linked by Zhukovsky and Goethe in the work "The Forest King", where a child during a trip in the night through the forest meets chthonic creatures, later taking his soul. Zhukovsky translated Goethe's ballad "The Forest King" in his own way. He deviated from the original, but his translation for the perfection of form was immediately recognized as exemplary. Zhukovsky's translation preserves the atmosphere of anxiety, premonition of doom, tragedy. The ballad is pervaded by fantasy, which is contained in the dialogues between the rider and his son, the son and the ghost that beckons him. The rider-father tries to give a reasonable explanation for his son's fears, but the mysterious visions and the voice of the forest king are stronger, and terror overwhelms the infant.

In the translation of the ballad "The Forest King" we hear the heartfelt voice of the narrator, who feels sorry for the sick child, who mistakes a feverish delusion for reality. Zhukovsky does not simply convey the conversation between father and son; he himself feels the child's fear and the father's powerlessness to help him.

Both Zhukovsky and Goethe depicted the fantastic power of inexplicable, mysterious phenomena that threaten man. But both poets allowed the possibility that the tragedy did not happen in real life, but only dreams, premonitions, therefore, fear is not omnipotent over man.

"Native, the king of the forest has summoned his daughters:

I see them nodding to me from the dark branches." -

"Oh no, all is calm in the depths of the night:

The gray branches stand aside."

"Child, I am captivated by your beauty:

Will or won't, you'll be mine." -

"Native, the king of the forest wants to catch up with us;

Here it is: I'm stuffy, I'm having trouble breathing."

Mikhail Bulgakov injected himself with morphine to fall into a state of chthonic twilight, learning there the essence of biblical plots and Satan's influence on the world, which formed the basis of his "Master and Margarita".

Remember N.V. Gogol with his works "Evenings on a Farm near Dikanka" and "Viy". His characters live as if in parallel worlds at the same time.

W.Shakespeare's Hamlet performs his deeds at a time when the others are in a state of rest - sleep. For them a day is 24 hours, but for Hamlet the night becomes a new stage of life.

Black Man S. Yesenin dictates the lines of the poem in the night, forcing the poet to plunge into the atmosphere of the chthonic twenty-four hours.

He sits on my bed,

Black man

Keeps me up all night.

Black man

Drives his finger through a nasty book

And, bellowing at me,

Like a dead monk,

Reading my life to me

Some hack and a hobo,

bringing fear and sadness to my soul.

Black man

Black, black!

The illustrations to the works under study, placed in the appendix, further emphasize the peculiarity of the poetic word in describing the images during the chthonic twenty-four hours. (see appendix).

The narrative chronotope of Homer's Odyssey

Within the framework of the method of obtaining a structural chronotope for Russian fairy tales proposed above, in this chapter we will obtain a spatial-temporal, calendar chronotope for the text of Odysseus' adventures recorded three thousand years ago. If in a myth we distinguish a plot chain of events connected only with the main hero, then much that we talked about at the beginning of the first chapter is applicable to the myth as well. In it we can also distinguish an oriented space of such events, in which both Zelinsky's law and the three basic laws of plot construction, which we used to construct the calendar chronotope of fairy tales, operate. Approaching the events in the epic as events in a sacralized, mythological space with fixed oriented twelve-month calendars, discussed below, we can schedule the entire text of the Odyssey narrative as follows.

The beginning of the narrative chain of events is fixed by the direction from the center of the ancient Greek world (Delphi) to Troy (where the main cult center of Ares, the god of war, was located). According to our event calendar this direction is for the conditional March-month. March (Ares-Mars) fixes the beginning of counting. Such binding of the spatial-event mythological calendar will show not only the time, but also the approximate direction (place) of a particular event of the narrative within the mythologem developed by the ancient Greeks. This allowed a literate Greek, who knew his myths and was privy to the mysteries of his mysteries, to be perfectly oriented in the topography of his native oikoumene.

Let us limit ourselves for the time being to the adventure part of the narrative, the main events of Odysseus' sea voyage.

CALENDAR CHRONOTOPE:

\0. The departure of Odysseus on 12 ships from Troy (March).\ 1. Island of Kikonov. Killing all the inhabitants. Escape. Storm at sea.\2. Nameless island. Storm. H. Lotus Island. Loss of memory from the lotus (drink of oblivion).\ 4. Goat Island. \ 5.Cyclops Island. Blinding Polyphemus. Insulting Poseidon. \6. Return to the ships at the island of Koz. \ 7. The island of Aeolus (Aeolus is the father of 12 children: 6 sons, 6 daughters). Zephyrus - west wind. Departure to Ithaca, sleep, envy of companions, opening of winds, passing Ithaca. Return to Aeolus. Insulting Aeolus. \ 8. The island of the Lestrygon giants. The loss of 11 ships. \9. The island of the sorceress Kirka (daughter of Helios). Beasts, acorns. 1 year as a guest of Kirky. The appearance of Hermes. Elpenor's death. \10. Odysseus in Hades (the northern country of the Cimmerians, the country of eternal night). Theresius' divination. Odysseus learns the reason for the disasters - Poseidon's revenge for his son, the Cyclops Polyphemus. \11. Return to the island of Kirki. Elpenor's funeral. Private predictions. \12. Island of the Sirens. Songs of Troy. \13. Scylla. The deaths of six satellites. \14. The island of Helios (Sun, son of Zeus). Storm. Famine. Violation of the ban and killing of the bulls of Helios. Escape from the island of Helios. Wind Zemphira, storm. Death of the last ship and companions who broke the ban and killed bulls. \15. South wind Notus. Charybdis. \16. Calypso Island. 7 years of memory loss. Zeus, Athena, and Hermes unchain Odysseus. 17. Poseidon's wrath, storm, Odysseus' raft wreck. \18. The island of King Alkinoi (of the Pheacians). Odysseus' victory in sports competitions. \19. Odysseus' return to Ithaca in a sleepy state. \20. Poseidon's anger at the Pheacians for breaking the ban and helping Odysseus. Odysseus and Athena. Odysseus' transformation into an old man. The gifts hidden in the cave.

Combining the events occurring within each conditional month into groups, we obtain the following series of conjugations. March: (0), sailing from Troy \ (12), sirens singing about Troy. April: (1), killing of part of the Kikonians \ (13), killing of part of the crew by Scylla. May: (2), unknown island, storm\ (14), Helios' island, storm, Zeus' revenge. June: (3), lotophagi, drink of forgetfulness from lotus\ (15), Charybdis, the river of forgetfulness of Summer in the calendar of the World of Hades, (16) Calypso, loss of memory. July: (5), the blinding of the Cyclops Polyphemus and his call to Poseidon for revenge\ (17), Poseidon sinks Odysseus' raft by storm and strips him. August: (6), Isle of Goats\ (18), Isle of Alkinoi (Pheakes), goddess Ino, September: (7), Isle of Aeolus (winds), storm, failure to reach Ithaca, Odysseus' return to Aeolus\ (19), Odysseus' return to Ithaca. For a preliminary check of the correctness of the chronotope of events in "The Odyssey" we can consider the following considerations as an argument. According to the main myth, the island of Cyclopes (5) and the island of Alkinoi \ island of the Pheacians; event (18)\ were neighboring ("Odyssey", song 6, verse 5), which caused much trouble to the Pheacians \II.23, p. 148\. 148\. Despite the fact that in the text of "The Odyssey" they are separated by a large interval of time and number of events, in the structure of the event chronotope we have obtained, they are still next to each other!

This is the manifestation of the cyclization of the plot inherent in this text. The reasons for such cyclization are in the calendar principle of the formation of the course of the narrative in epic, myth, fairy tale.

The following events are grouped by three:

(Scylla/ Helio-sa/Charybdis island); (Aeolus/ Ithaca/Eolus) and (Pheacus/Ithaca/the punishment of the Pheacians). Here the moment of Odysseus' return to Aeolus after untying the bag of winds is important. If in the first event loop Odysseus does not get to Ithaca (he sailed past Ithaca), then in the second event loop this moment corresponds to the arrival of the sleepy Odysseus to Ithaca (his incomplete return), and the incomplete return of the Pheacians to their island - Poseidon turned them into a Rock. The episode with Kirka (events 9-11) can be considered a similar group of events: (Kirka\Aid\Kirka). Thus, the events grouped by triplets divide the event field into three parts (Heli-os\Itaka/Aid). This constitutes the main triad in the piece of text under consideration. According to the above systematization, the chain of events (event chronotope) is divided into three sectors. In the first spring-summer sector everything is grouped around Helios the Sun, the son of Zeus. It is characterized by the period of voyages and risky adventures. In the second sector (summer-autumn) events are grouped around the god of winds Aeolus and Poseidon. The time of feasts, festivals, gifts and sports games (see above the analysis of the myth about Theseus and his establishment of the Isthmian games in September: the time of the visit to the island of Pheacus and Odysseus' participation in sports competitions is also September! - event 18.). The third group of events (winter) includes visits to the world of ancestors (Hades), conversion into animals, sleep, and the time of prophecies and divination.

The coincidence of the chronotope of events in different myths (here: the coincidence of the time of sports games in the myths of Odysseus and Theseus) is not accidental, but a reflection of a steadily existing religious and ritual tradition.

Another interesting coincidence: according to the event calendar, the moment of Odysseus' visit to King Alcinoi and the competition in which Odysseus participated coincides with the time of the Delphic Games (September). The text of the Odyssey even lists the main types of competitions in this episode: running, wrestling, jumping, fist fighting, discus throwing. It seems to us that this literal binding of the text to the annual mythological calendar was the motivation for the appearance of the episode of sports competitions in the text. According to our observation, there are no other motives (and reasons for the long preservation of this episode in the oral tradition). Finally, we note that the moment of the slaughter of the bulls of Helios (event 14 in Fig. 11.1.A) falls on the month of May according to our event calendar of the narrative. In relation to the Peloponnesian peninsula this corresponds to the direction to the island of Crete (the ancient Greek cult center of Helios the bull. This cult itself was brought from Egypt, which is in the same geographical direction from Mycenae).

It should also be noted that the three events connected with the visit of the Cyclops Polyphemus to the unnamed island (4) - Polyphemus' island (5) - unnamed island (6)\ emphasize Polyphemus as a carrier of the chthonic obstacle, a man-eater. Close to this episode is the event (17) - Poseidon's revenge for the blinding of Polyphemus' son. On the other hand, Odysseus' visit to the island of lotophagi (3) with drinking juice from the lotus infusion and Odysseus' stay on the island of Calypso (16) coincide on the calendar of the World of Hades with the moment of crossing the river of oblivion of Summer and with the month of Hypnos (July) - the son of Nykta (Night). These events lie on the axis of spring/autumn transition (see Appendix-3, the ancient Greek calendar).

Similarly on the axis of transition autumn/winter there is an event of destruction of almost all ships \ 11 out of 12 ships were destroyed and eaten by giants - Lestrogonians (8). But it is the month that marks the end of the year. The transition from winter to spring corresponds to the moment of departure from Troy (event \0.) and the visit to the island of the Sirens (songs of the Sirens about Troy, event \ 12.). Thus, according to the text, at these moments of the event year human sacrifices were made to the chthonic forces. The destruction of the ship in the event (event \ 14.) is not connected not with natural forces, but with the violation of the prohibition to kill the bulls of Helios. Such division of the annual circle into three main seasons with sacrifices during the transitions between them is a peculiarity of the ancient Greek (Mediterranean) cult tradition.

In terms of the dialectic of the development of categories, we can see that the opposition (departure/return) from Ithaca dialectically passes through the following phases in the course of the narrative: (not getting to Ithaca (7)\, incomplete return to Ithaca (19)\, final return (25)). It should be noted that the episode of Teresius' main prediction (the event \10.) falls in January (holy days), which according to modern beliefs is the most optimal time for such divinations.

The moments of appearance in the text of the main gods taking part in the fate of the main character of the Odyssey are not accidental. Thus, Boreas appears in April, Cyclops Polyphemus (son of Poseidon) in August, Aeolus (October), Kirka (daughter of Helios) in December, she cannot appear earlier, because according to the text, she feeds the travelers turned into pigs with acorns, and they ripen. according to the text she feeds acorns to the travelers turned into pigs, and they ripen by November\ and in February; Hades (in January?); Ares (in March); Helios (in May); Not-South Wind (in June!), Poseidon (July, August, October, December-January). By the way, December at Greeks was so called - Poseidonius). The main initiators of the intrigue Zeus and Athena appear in the text: Zeus (in June he drowned the ship and the desecrators of Helios' bulls, \ in July he freed Odysseus from Calypso (16)); Athena (April, July, August, September and further), When analyzing the system of conjugations we used the following ancient Greek mythological and cult calendars: Zeus' World Calendar.

\1. Ares.

\Athena (April, wisdom, nature)

\3. Aphrodite (May, beauty and love)

\4. Hera (June, beauty, marriage, birth)

\5. Zeus (July, mind, law, order)

\6. Hephaestus (August, fire, earthquakes, crafts)

\7. Hestia (September, home and purifying fire, weddings)

\8. Hades (October, the world of the dead, underground)

\19.Demerta (November, fertility of the land)

\10. Artemis (December, patroness of animals, hunting).

\11.Poseidon (January, waters of the earth, sea).

\12.Apollo (February, light radiating,).

Aida's World Calendar.

\1. Underworld (the land of unburied souls).

\2 Charon (river. Styx). \3\ Cerberus.

\Minos (judge of the buried).

\4. Persephone (the land of unquenched souls and plant spirits).

\5. Hecate (the fork in the road to Tartarus or Hades).

\6.Mania (mani-dom, the paradise of the righteous).

\7. The River of Summer (island of the blessed, oblivion).

\Nykta (Hypnos, Thanatos, Night).

\Hades (fire of purification).

Let us return to the episodes connected with the sorceress Kirka. In the first episode (December) she plays the role of Artemis (the hunter, patroness of animals and livestock), to whom sacrifices are made at the beginning of December, and in the second episode (after Odysseus returns from Hades) she plays the role of Apollo - Phebus \ twin of Artemis \ who is the patron of February and is able to predict the future \because of this quality was founded in Delphi (northeast of Athens) dedicated to him a sanctuary for predictions \ ...

The calendar of the World of Zeus coincides with the zodiacal calendar if the last to turn "back" on 48 days. If to use tables of the World circle then we receive the following interesting coincidences concerning calendar of Zeus and zodiacal calendar. As one zodiacal month corresponds to 2160 years, we will receive that 3456 years ago (in 1456 BC) on January 1 came the first year of Aquarius era, which is associated with the god Poseidon as the keeper of underground waters. Then on October 1 (or the day of the autumnal equinox) falls Scorpio - the symbol of Hades (three-headed Cerberus with a poisonous dragon's tail, and on July 1 falls the sign of Leo (the symbol of Zeus, which coincides with the month of Zeus). Namely, it is possible to assert that the calendar of the World of Zeus (ancient Greek calendar of Homer) somehow is connected with more ancient (Indo-European) zodiacal calendar. Ancient Hebrew lunar religious calendar, which begins with the month of Aviv (Nisan, March), can be considered close to the considered calendar. On the day of the full moon of this month (15 Nisan) the Passover is celebrated (originally it was the day of harvest, and later it was considered to be the day of exodus from Egypt). Exactly 6 lunar months later, after the Day of Purification, the Feast of Tabernacles is celebrated (15 Afanim, September). Forty-five days before Passover, the beginning of the month of Adar (February 1st according to the lunar calendar) is celebrated. In the ancient Greek tradition, it was this day that was dedicated to Apollo (Phoebus). As applied to the later Orthodox tradition, Pancake Day was timed to this day (7 weeks before Easter). Thus, Pancake Day can also be considered in connection with the

Delphic Mysteries (festivals of light) dedicated to Apollo.

It should be noted that in the Tibetan calendar to this day (the end of the first full lunar month after the winter solstice) the beginning of the New Year is timed and the day of cleansing from the spirits of the old year is celebrated (dolls-mulagi are burned), etc. So it is possible that there are also Far Eastern elements in the Shrovetide ritual tradition. So the ritual tradition of Pancake Day can also include Far Eastern elements.

It should be noted that the calendar year in the Hebrew lunar calendar began with the 7th month of Afanim (or Tishri, September). It should be emphasized that on the 50th day after the Jewish Passover (after the seventh day) the day of the Law (Moses) was celebrated. One of calendar triads in the considered calendar is (Day of the Law / Day of purification / Shebat (January)). The second triad (Passover, the Day of Tuvalcain (Elul, Elijah Day), the Day of the Temple (25 Kislev, Hanukkah)). If to compare with the ancient Greek calendar, the pre-biblical holiday Tuvalkain (day of Cain, copper, smiths) coincides with the Day of Hephaestus.

The calendar of the World of Hades is reconstructed from Virgil's Aeneid. It is nine-month, contains 40 days in a conventional month and is not tied to lunar cycles. According to the Greeks, such a calendar determined the special pull of underground time, the slow intensity of chthonic forces. We have chosen a calendar from another literary source to show its effectiveness for the case under consideration. On the other hand, for the initial analysis of the text we made preliminary calendars, less detailed, but consistent with the given ones, using the above-mentioned oppositions. That is, for the preliminary analysis of the text, the text itself is sufficient without the involvement of extra-textual material.

In the "underworld", the shadow (the human soul weighed down by life) waits for 40 days for the burial of the body, during which it is given a coin to pay Charon for traveling across the Styx and a flatbread for Cerberus. The crowd of transported shadows is waiting for the trial by lot at Minos. After the trial, some of the shadows, the souls who have not yet calmed down from their earthly life and are suffering about their earthly life, fall to Persephone, who has the opportunity to go to the surface of the Earth in March and help those living on Earth at the request of the dead (4). Between the events (5) and (6) the pacified shadow, following its fate, or by the decision of Persephone or Hecate, falls either into the palace of Hades (6), or into Tartarus \transition to another half-plane\. Behind the palace of Hades there is the river Leta, those who swim across it get to the Island of the Blessed (the Island of Oblivion).

In terms of studying the later borrowing of elements of the myth of Hades in Russian fairy tales, the invisibility of Hades and Persephone for the heroes visiting Hades is connected with the fact that Hades possessed a golden magic helmet making him invisible (invisible hat) and copper sandals instantly moving him to any place (speed boots). These magical aids he gave to Persephone every year when she came to the surface to Demeter in early March. This made her invisible to Cerberus.

We dwell so much on the mythological calendars of early Hellenism rather than on the Greek cult calendars of the period of Hesiod and Homer because the surviving texts of the Odyssey and the Illiad were reworked in the 1st century B.C. in accordance with the then later ideas about the world (Alexandrian lists). Overlaying the calendars cited on the event chronotope of the Odyssey, we can easily find many interesting parallels and juxtapositions.

Many identified features in the text of "The Odyssey" can be explained if we imagine that within a single episode there is an overlap of events from different calendars (the World of Zeus, the World of Hades, the World of Poseidon, the real World) corresponding to it in terms of chronotope, the possibility of the appearance of which we have identified above when analyzing Russian fairy tales.

Thus, it is easy to establish that the events "sleep at the nymph Calypso" and "intoxication with lotus", rather separated from each other in the text, but appearing close in the event calendar (structural chronotope), are connected with the coinciding with them conditional month of the god Gynozos (July) in the calendar of the World of Hades. But it was Hypnozos who was responsible for sleep, lulling, oblivion, which took place in these events. The appearance of the story with the Cyclops Polyphemus can be explained by the fact that in the calendar of the World of Poseidon at this time of year falls a month dedicated to the third, younger Cyclops - the son of Poseidon, (according to other versions - he is an assistant to Hephaestus - aus. August - in the forge).

Reading "The Odyssey" we find the episode "Souls of bridegrooms in the kingdom of Hades", where the use of such a calendar is explicitly stated: "The souls of bridegrooms followed Hermes along the gloomy road in a string. He led them further and further, past the waters of the gray Ocean (north), past the gates of the sun god Helios (east), past the country where the gods of sleep live (Hypnozos, south), past the rock Leucada (west, the entrance to Hades)". I.e., the souls of the murdered bridegrooms made a full calendar circle in the World of Hades.

On the other hand, this paragraph actually gives a brief retelling of the whole plot of Odysseus' journey. This is a rather interesting method of compiling the plot of a legend: to see different mythological calendars and choose the appropriate episode corresponding to a given aus. month.

Based on this assumption, we can even calculate the average event time of Odysseus' journey. Thus, according to the text, he spent 7 years with the nymph Calypso, 1 year with the sorceress Kirky, and according to the event chronotope he actually spent 1.5 conventional years to arrive in Ithaca. Total -9,5 conditional years.

Thus, we see that the structure of the calendar chronotope, in addition to the external form of the narrative plot, is also a kind of cipher of cult, mystery calendars, and a certain topographical map of some real journey. Apparently, this is how Heinrich Schliemann, the discoverer of Troy, imagined it all, when he searched for its location literally following the text of the Illiad: using the map of ancient Hellas and following the cult places of Ares.

The afterlife world in the form of a meadow-pasture with burnt sacrificial animals was called uellu (Elysian meadows, the meadows of Veles, the cattle god) by the Indo-Europeans. Is not the story of the king Elisha, as the lord of the afterlife, matchmaking for the Sleeping Princess (nature) - like a fairy-tale version of the myth of Persephone and Hades? Such a predilection of Proto-Indo-Europeans once again reminds us of a possible ancestral homeland - the meadow steppes of Donbas.

In the analysis of the fairy tale "Geese - Swans" we dwelled on the surprising coincidence in the chronotope of events of the moment of the appearance of storms in various ancient Greek myths. In "The Odyssey" it refers to the spring season and events (\2. - the storm at the beginning of the sailing from Troy, \14. - the storm near the island of Helios) and the autumn storms connected with Odysseus' approach to Ithaca (events \7. - the storm near the island of Aeolus and \19. - the storm on Odysseus' return). This coincides with the fact of the change of direction of the Mediterranean monsoon (ethesia) off the coast of Greece. A closer look at this motif in "The Odyssey" and in the myth of the Argonauts analyzed below reveals a stable repetition of the opposition: the heroes' departure in spring \ their arrival at the beginning of winter. This corresponds to the seasonal direction of the monsoon-ettesia: in summer it blows steadily from north to south, and in winter - from south to north. Therefore, in summer you can sail safely from Attica to the islands (most are located southeast of mainland Greece), and in winter, with full sails, hurry home with the spoils. This is such an annual cycle of deployment of the opposition of sailing return and arises when analyzing these myths. By the way, the reader can see for himself that the seasonal and mythological calendars given in Appendix-3 take into account this most serious factor of ancient Greek culture (in the ancient Greek pantheon there were both northern and southern winds, and the god of storms of transitional seasons /the same Aeolus/).

Chthonic motifs in the legend of Vseslav Polotsky

The famous retelling of Boyan's "songs" about Vseslav Polotsk, included in the text of "The Tale of Igor's Campaign", has repeatedly attracted the attention of various researchers who tried to clarify the historical background of certain episodes, to restore the sequence and causes of real events or to restore the general complex of ideas about the mysterious prince-turned-king. It should be noted that in most cases the "dark places", possible variants of their interpretations and corrections were in the center of attention, while the clear, only to a small extent studied mythological layer remained outside the study.

First of all, this refers to the extremely rare in Old Russian literature (especially in such an early time) references to the deities of the chthonic pantheon, the memory of which was intensively erased by the church. The purpose of this note is to show the possibility of a mythological reading of a controversial fragment of the legend of Vseslav. It is about the phrase:

"Vseslav the prince judges the people, the princes row the towns, and he himself in the night trotting far and wide; from Kyev he reached Kury Tmutorokan; to the great Khrsov the way was interrupted far and wide".

In this fragment, the constant attention of modern researchers is attracted by the combination "up to Kur'kur'Tmutorokan", where "up to Kur'kur" acts as a spatial reference point, or a temporal reference point. In the first case, the word is defined as a toponym, in which researchers see the city of Kursk, the Kura River, or Turkism ("up to the walls - or towers - of Tmutorokan"); in the other case - an indication of the time of day ("up to the singing of roosters"). Consideration of this expression not in isolation, but in context, taking into account the graphic features reproduced in the first edition of 1800 and repeated in the famous "Catherine's copy", allows, in our opinion, to propose another possible interpretation.

Two points seem to be the most important: the connection of "Kura" with Vseslav's nocturnal werewolfing, when Vseslav "to the great Hrsovi" (the sun in its night hypostasis, as opposed to Dazhd-god, the daytime sun) "the way interrupted" (i.e., outstripped), and the stable spelling of Kura with a capital letter as a proper name or title. The retention of this spelling in both the Catherine copy and the first edition, which is forgotten by subsequent publishers and commentators of The Tale of Igor's Campaign, suggests that in the manuscript original the capital letters were distinguished either by pale cinnabar or by their bolder lettering, and numerous copyists kept the spelling, In contrast to "Khors", which lost not only its original meaning but also its individual graphic characteristic over the centuries, as a result of which it was reproduced in the first edition with a lowercase initial "x".

In other words, the above-mentioned features allow us, abstracting from the toponym "Tmutorokan", on which the commentators concentrate their attention, to present "Kur" as a certain mythical creature that was part of the system of representations "night-sun-underworld". The above three components, despite their small number, have the merit that together they outline the circle of mythological consciousness in which "Kur" can exist and, to a certain extent, define this enigmatic image.

Both Vseslav's nocturnal werewolfism and the mention of Khors inevitably lead us to that part of the mythological representations of various peoples, which centers around the most important aspect of the solar myth: the night journey of the day luminary, his dying and resurrection in the waters of the underworld, his descent at sunset into the realm of the dead. It is difficult to overestimate the role played by the ideas about the "lower world" and the cult of chthonic deities in the life of cultural peoples of antiquity. Without even attempting to cover in general terms the complex variety of cults, mysteries and images on which the dualistic comprehension of "life-death", "microcosm-macrocosm", etc. was based, it is worth noting that the chthonic characters, shrouded in the mystery of darkness, in the representations of antiquity and the Middle Ages were much more important for everyday life than their daytime antithesis, or rather just their daytime hypostases. This dualism, elaborated in detail in the religious doctrines and cults of the Indo-Iranian world, most fully embodied in Zoroastrianism, in the European Middle Ages found favorable ground among heretical sects, of which in southern Europe the Cathars and Albigoyans were the most famous, and in eastern Europe the Bogumils (Bulgaria), whose works were circulated in Russia, falling into the indexes of "renounced" books.

Partly published, but still insufficiently studied, these "renounced" works, circulating in Russia already in pre-Mongol times, have preserved traces and retellings of the most ancient myths of the Near and Middle East, going back from the civilizations of Anatolia and Dvurechia to the followers of Zoroaster, and from them - through the Armenians - to the Bogomils. One of such reflections of the most ancient solar myth is the "Tale of the Great Kur", which is a part of the little-studied "Tale of the Whole Creation" and is better known under the name "The Word about the Trinity on the Creation of Heaven and Earth". It is mentioned in the Solovetsky indexes of "renounced" books, published in his time by N.S. Tikhonravov from a list from the Collection No. 774 of 153119 and is contained in the Collection of the 16th century of the collection of the Historical Museum, where the most complete text of the "Tale of the Great Kur" reads on fol. 137: "... The sun flows through the air in the daytime, and at night through the ocean low-flying, but then it is washed in the ocean three times a day," says the writing. And the sea is the head of the earth up to the sky, and the sea is the head of the earth up to the col[e]n. The sun is washed in the ocean, then the ocean will be all inclusive. And the sea waves will begin to beat the kura on the feathers of the kura, and the kura, having honored the sea waves, will also sing, O Lord God, and give light to the world. Then all the chickens will sing in one year. In the whole universe the sun will be removed from the akiyan, the ocean from the sun, and all the waters from the akiyan.

The "Kur'u" represented in this text, as can be seen, meets exactly those features that were outlined above, when analyzing the text about Vseslav and Khors: it is located near the waters of the world ocean (i.e. in the underworld), where the sun descends in the evening, and "regulates" the path of the daylight in the night, being connected with the sun and the night by a direct relationship.

However, at the moment we are more interested in another aspect of the Tale, its real content, thanks to which the figure of one of the chthonic deities with a pronounced zoomorphic appearance appears before us, transformed under the pen of the Russian scribe from an inhabitant of the underworld (the kingdom of the dead, the ocean of the dead) into a kind of ultimate reference point of the conceivable world. It is in this way - to Kur, ad ultima Thule - to the extreme limits of the existing world, "to the last sea", that the prince-turned-prince Vseslav reaches, outrunning the night sun in his run.

And he is not the only one. The attempt to trace the origins of the "Tale", reflected in such an unusual way in "The Tale of Igor's Campaign" through the retelling of the legend of Vseslav (it is legitimate to ask the question: Polotsk, or all-Slavic?), takes us to the depths of Indo-Iranian mythology, at the origins of which we find Sumerian clay tablets with records of the poem about Gilgamesh and the goddess Inanna patronizing the hero.

Dostoevsky's cosmos

Dostoevsky was studied: his thoughts and characters; his ideology; his psychology as a psychologist of the human soul; the structure of his novels (polyphony and dialogism - according to M. M. Bakhtin). The corporeality, matter, and subject matter of his world somehow remained unattended[1] . Is it all without significance that he has a city, a cheese, white nights, no animals, kitchens, corners, partitions, spiders, stench, staircases, consumption, epilepsy, no mothers, no fathers, no births, no Caucasus, no sea, but ponds? I.e. not only what there is, but also minuscule materiality, i.e. things that he does not have and that other Russian writers have and that are significant in the context of Russian literature - all this is also voice and meaning. And this materiality is not just a filler of the structure - no, it is ideological, it is also a full-fledged voice in the polyphony of the Whole. For bodies, things are not spiritually mediocre, but they are co-constituted with spiritual meanings, they are body-ideas.

We will read Dostoevsky's Cosmos (in the Hellenic sense - as the structure of the world) in the ancient natural philosophical language of the four elements.

Why does Dostoevsky have no nature and landscapes, but everything is concentrated in the city, and what could this mean? Nature is native to us. There is no alienation here. In the midst of nature, man's sense of his peculiarity and uniqueness in being dissolves - something that is acutely encircled in the city, since man there is the only living, nature-born creature - an organism in the midst of an artificial world of mechanisms - surrounding, but not native (for he is not born in the gony, but created by labor in the gurgia)[2] . Dostoevsky needs this excommunication from nature in order, having broken the umbilical cord with the fraternal environment, to short-circuit people only on each other, thus creating a huge tension, a vibrator, an amplifier for looking at the slightest intra-human mental strivings[3] .He needs the city as a matter of principle in order to find a man without other relatives in existence, except for his own kind: only the human race is his kin, not nature - and that is why he has a monoteme: man and the fate of mankind in the vacuum of lifelessness and in the foreign land of substance. Tolstoy, on the contrary, takes inter-human tensions to the sky (Prince Andrei's Austerlitz) and to the earth (the blade of grass in the chorus to "Resurrection"). He has

[1]

[2]

humanity disconnected into nature = the native. In him, and in Pushkin, in whom nature was also included in the range of the worldview, existence is more comprehensive, but also more relaxed, for there are more substances, species = ideas, objects. In Dostoevsky, there are no vistas, no unseen (fog, night), no external spaces (landscapes), but the world of forces and energies wanders apart from the masses. With him, as in dynamics, force and time are the categories. He creates the dynamics of Psyche, the World Soul in its incarnation into a human soul, in the middle of Cosmos (the world of God, which he does not accept - cf. Ivan Karamazov) and Logos (reason, "Arithmetic"). And in isolation from space, the attribution of oneself to the current of time is equally intensified. (This is why, by the way, the time of action in his novels is enlarged so much: the whole drama is almost completed in one day, half of "The Idiot" - in one night).

But to deny the assistance and complicity of space in Russia - the land of spaces (cf. Gogol: "what does this vast expanse prophesy?") - is truly an incomprehensible sacrilege: it is the light and snow that has been encroached upon and overshadowed by their innards, their entrails - human souls. [3]And this Dostoevsky blasphemy against the "Russian God" (which, in Pushkin's words, in "The Storm of the Twelfth Year" "helped us") is comparable only to Peter the Great's = stone violence against natural Russia, when he cut it down, shortened it and drove it into a stone hail on the marshes, creating the mythologeme of water and stone as a new plot of Russian history (listen to it in "The Bronze Horseman" and "The Iron Stream"). That is why Dostoevsky organically needs St. Petersburg as the navel of his world, the center of the Psycho-Cosmo-Logos in the Dostoevskian way. Even in Cheremoshnya and in Russian country towns, he goes out with the texture of Petersburg, like Nicholas the Wonderworker with a city-temple on his arm: the same Petersburg weather (fogs, rains, slushy snow) and cramped streets, houses, halls and fences - analogous to city walls.

In the midst of nature there is naturalness and ease in man. In the city - freedom and (or) necessity. In nature, there is a pre- and non-subject-object dissection of being and man, a pre-Kantian, pre-Dostoevsky[5] stay in natural ("dogmatic") trust, in the unity and syncretism of being and thinking: there is no criticism yet, and the epistemological problem has not yet arisen, unlike ontology.

And here it is, Kant's revolt of Hippolytus in The Idiot: "What do I need your nature..., your sunrises and sunsets, your blue sky..." (the main antagonists of Dostoevsky's world are listed: the sky and the sun. Dostoevsky has no sky: he is turned away to the nooks and crannies of the city, his gaze is downward and oblique. There is no sun: neither as light nor as eyes in the sky - only "the slanting rays of the setting..." Well, yes, his favorite white nights are a sunless mareva of light, an eyeless light, a veil, an eyesore of the hidden polar sun. It is light without its subject, atheistic light), when all this feast to which there is no end (and this is a hostile idea: infinity, for it is a dissipation, an opponent of the force that gains itself precisely in the measure of the condensation, the finiteness of (non-) being into being, thing, life singular. So the mortality and finitude of man is a precondition for his becoming an energetic clot of forces and the arena of their dynamics. Being is driven into a corner in man - the basic geometric figure in Dostoevsky - and there, in its trap, where it has nowhere to go, it is forced to confess in confession, its secrets are squeezed out of Psyche, she is pulsating and panting - in the novel as on the screen. And to stage this experiment such a camera obscura as Dostoevsky's St. Petersburg is created), started with the fact that he considered me alone as an extra?"[6] Here is the key phrase. But it's the other way around: it's not me that nature threw out, but I rejected it, a self-deprived person. But by this sacrifice, in this act of cutting the umbilical cord, I get my Descartesian "I", on which everything will be built further on. It was not the world-feast that began with the fact that I alone was considered superfluous, but I (the character of Dostoevsky's world, and its demiurge, God the Creator-Author) began with the fact that the world was considered superfluous ("I do not accept God's world").

So the cut is from nature, from the mother(s), for nature, as birth, is the mother. City is masculine, father. Nature is feminine, mother. So it is not without reason that urban civilization occurs under patriarchy. And as Dostoevsky's novel develops, the disappearance of the image of the mother and the build-up of the image of the father are clearly traceable. In "Poor People" a lot more space is occupied by Varvara's mother, her calamities, the father is unknown, and the second father - Pokrovsky - is ridiculous, and is hinted at only by the father on' big Bykov (and the Bull is not the constellation of Virgo, under which our Blessed - Makar[7] Devushkin). And to his beloved sister Makar is addressed by the words "matochka" = mat(y + dev)oka, constriction. In "Crime and Punishment" there are mothers, and this novel is transitional, belongs still to the traditional, monological, European. In "Adolescence" the mother pales, the father is important. In "The Brothers Karamazov" the father grows to half the sky, half the world, and the mother is reduced to a rag of Elizaveta Smidyaschaya.

What is a man in the city, from the point of view of the elements? The correspondence of "Poor People" is the chirping of the city's sparrows, which sit in the windows of some floors and echo with each other across the courtyard, discussing human affairs in a human voice. He calls her "bird", "birdie", "dove", "angel", dreams of making a nest or is going to fly away, but in the end he feels himself as a chick that has fallen out of a broken nest. And although Makarovo gives Varvara the religious-literary stamp of an exhortation to live like the birds of God, it is not without reason that he spoke about it and contrasted himself with the image of a certain "bird of prey". They are not birds of prey, but they are also birds of prey!.. In their names one can hear a certain melancholic "carr", and the whole climate around them is gray-sky, inherent in these melancholic birds, and all that they see misfortunes ahead and misfortunes behind, so it is better not to remember.

But there is much in this self-comparison of our poor people with birds - not with a horse, as in Tolstoy (Holstomer, Anna - comparison with Frou-Frou), not with a plant (Andrei's oak, Murat's burdock, the birch - the barmaid - "Three Deaths"). All Tolstoy's pairs of people are heavy, full of earth, weighty life, growing from below. The bird is an inhabitant of the element of air. Already by this a certain Credo is declared: I confess not the element of earth, water, fire (although air will have a complicated plot with all of them), but a light nature. Even the negative creatures here are insects, abundant in Dostoevsky: cockroaches, spiders (that light of Svidrigailov's), "am I a louse or Napoleon?", "an old lady louse". All of them are not strong on earth, inhabitants of the same intermediate space between heaven and earth as birds.

In general, every person here feels like a spider in his soul: he weaves the web, the fabric of life, and is entangled and oppressed by it. And the movements of the characters are not smooth, flexible, rounded, like those of the great creatures of earth and water, but angular, convulsive, like lights, their trajectory zigzagging, like those of insects: Raskolnikov remains motionless in the corner of the coffin for a long time in place, then darts back and forth, scattering and multiplying his corner in space (he does not even loop after the crime: the loop is too rounded for him, an animal-like geometrical figure, but it is Raskolnikov who angles, (ra) splits!). And the energies are all discrete: he lies down, he kills, he hides, then suddenly he bursts into tears, he reveals himself in confession. No, the earthly existence here is not serious, not weighty, punctuated, but there is a certain abuse of air over our existing existence, its seriousness, measures, concerns and values. For these souls are not dense, not strong in incarnation. Here they meet from the world in the third-class carriage, the demon Rogozhin and the angel Myshkin, both sent for the time being for mankind (as for localism) - and the plot of recognitions, reveals begins, in the course of which one totality, which came together with Lev Nikolayevich's wedge, is recognized with another, which came from the underground of the Manichean black sun and bent an angle on Parfyon Rogozhin. And in general, the whole matter of existence is here - with a gash, climbing and sprawling, like the uniform and boots of Dostoevsky's officials, which cover shame, laughter and sin - ajar, and sucking in, and enticing, and sharpening the eye on it.

Air is also connected with the unusual sensitivity to odors in the apartment descriptions: the smoke, the fumes of the kitchens, the stench of the stairwells. By the way, the staircases, so important to Dostoevsky, are birds' perches and the staves of people suspended in cages in the air. And the city mystically beckons him because here the element of earth is raised, airy in the gaps of the rooms and voids, its thickness is not so hopelessly material and weighty, but it is already masculine and spiritualized. Spirit and air are indeed Dostoevsky's first but distant homeland in the cosmos, and now, perhaps, he does not even need pure air, but let him breathe in a corner of the kitchen with the smoke and cinders of earthly life. For this air is oriented not to the top (the sky and the sun), but to the bottom, the captive spirit, the air in love, is magnetically enchanted by it. It's like the angels in the Bible that looked to love human wives - and couldn't. There is in Dostoevsky's cosmos a voluptuousness for man, for him to be full of weight - and nemogota, because the angel-demon is light, spiritual, everything bubbles upwards out of its weight. So he pushes himself down, squirms, drives himself into the underground, and takes on himself all the blacks, guilt and sins, in order to humiliate himself and become like people, - but no, his ears, that is, his wings stick out: he can't be truly embodied, so he jumps in a panic attack; like a chicken is not a bird, a character of Dostoevsky is not a man. That is why everything crucifies him: then he goes backwards, upwards, into mankind-gods, then downwards into demons, but he does not get a full-body human being. The texture of the human fabric is stretched on Dostoevsky's loom and shines through. And man himself is a ball (his favorite hypostasis of the ball of the Whole - as not densely uninterrupted, but discretely woven out of waves-nitey-lives). Sin is necessary, greedy, for it is only through it that the demon-spirit can become stronger, lowered, weighted with phlogiston, springing upwards after each grounding. That is why lowly nature and all kinds of dirt and cinders, evil and crime are so beloved here - for they are not looked at from below, but from the top of inaccessibility, whence the human lot is close - but you can't bite it. So all these Raskolnikovs, going to the crime, do not want to become Napoleons, they have an inner goal, - but exactly human beings, an old woman, a louse; and the image of Napoleon and superman is a course, as we take it on a distant object, in order to reach the place we need in the middle. So Dostoevsky has it: the subhumans of the light take a course to the superhuman of the bottom, the villain, in order to reach the man and settle down in him. The thirst for life is great in unfulfilled airs. The merely living, in whom life is calm, have no thirst for life, for they have life-water with them. But these have a thirst for the heat of life. They lack fire, and fire is obtained by friction, so they rub themselves against people and love the warmth of irritation and suffering. They rush into the clatter, crackle, and jostle of people. (Did Makar choose a corner in the kitchen for nothing? Here he warms himself near life and tints his anemia.) They need a city, for a city = gor-gary, fire. City = stone fire: look at the texture of the city - the whole city is bursting with tongues of stone flame: houses, skyscrapers, churches, spires. And this is how the element of fire is represented in Dostoevsky's space. Like moths, the unfulfilled airs reach out to him. But since there is not enough flesh - earth-jacket on them and it is in gaps, it quickly burns out, and their substance - air - begins to burn. And this is consumption - the main disease of spiritual heroes. That is why, on the other hand, they need raw material: autumn, rain, slush - for irrigation and cooling, like a water jacket to the engine. In summer, they burn up completely, they go mad, (Ippolit's suicide attempt is in summer), like fish on sand. So, by the thirst of the unfulfilled airs for earth, water and fire, it is clear why they have condensed themselves to live in that place of the planet where the raw material is great (the Neva marshes) and the earth is hard ("The Neva is clothed in granite": "Petersburg" is literally "a fortress of stone")[8] , and where the friction of people against each other in the crowdedness of hired apartments is great and, consequently, the social fire burns strongly (the contrasts of wealth and poverty, arrogance and humiliation, bondage and longing for freedom).

What is the plot of this dialog (St. Petersburg - Russia) from the natural philosophical point of view, if it is expressed through the elements? Rus = mother raw earth, so it is watery land. But it is so in summer. In winter it is "wind-wind and white snow": there is neither water nor land. Snow is light. So, Russia is a werewolf, a dialog of two hypostases of itself: female - in summer (living life, spring) and male - in winter (Frost - wind-water people-light). And so they live and love each other, alternately ruling in the Psycho-CosmoLogos as day and night; and winter here is day, husband, the realm of whiteness and light, then Uranus-sky overturns on the earth, inseminating it with stars-snowflakes; and summer is darkness, greenery, life - wife (or, in the spiritual-erotic version, "my sister life"). And suddenly, into this factory and warehouse, into the established rhythm of Russia, Peter threw a boulder-stone, - and around him the crystallization of the solution of the mother's raw earth began. A new man appeared, a rival of Frost, Kesar against Svetra-people. There was an older nation, and now there is a smaller nation.

So, in the elements: fire-stone on water against wind and light - that's what St. Petersburg is in Russia. And the floods of the Neva are the uprisings of the oppressed mother raw earth, pressed down by the stone on the Chukhonian bogs, from which the blood-water in it went up to flood the surface - together with the wind:

It is the same in the revolution: when the people went to Peter, - then "wind-wind and white snow" bursts into the city of stone. But the stone takes the water-life into captivity and shuts up the wind: there is no place for it to swing among the walls and nooks and crannies to "open up, shoulder!", and now the water is blackness and swampy stench, standing, a crowd of self-righteous bourgeoisie that begins to teach the poet = the wind:

- both are humiliated together, the poet and the wind - and the blacks offer the wind to serve as a garbage man in the streets of the city (to cleanse the vices of the crowd).

If Fyodor Pavlovich Karamazov is Kronos, chthonic, then in the structure of the novel his analogous light hypostasis in terms of transcendence is the elder Zosima. However, he too may have been Karamazov (= Chernomazy, i.e. the devil, Beelzebub) in the past, a great sinner (there are hints of this, and his corpse stank of Karamazov's rottenness) - but he is the one whose transformation the heavens rejoice over, for he clutches a lot of life and dirt into the light and the heavens, and raises it up, powerfully enlightening matter, like a bodhisattva. So Father Karamazov is perhaps halfway to Zosima. That Mitya is like this - already three quarters of the way to Zosima - is very obvious.

And it turns out that the "Life of the Great Sinner" is realized by Dostoevsky in The Brothers Karamazov, but not monologically (as he conceived of a series of novels that should have consistently depicted the path of one character, say, Alyosha) - to this he was incapable, as M. M. Bakhtin has shown. M. Bakhtin, was incapable of it - but in such a way that different stages and branches of this path, different episodes and hypostases of this Vita are deployed in simultaneity - and they are realized by the chorus and polyphony of all the characters and situations. So this is the Mass, the Passion according to Theodore[4] - and precisely in his inherent dialogic, incomplete, open and questioning manner. To the same, titanic, level belong Svidrigailov, Stavrogin, Versilov, but they are all drier and more social, more flat.

Stavrogin is more the fire of hell, Lucifer (Latin for light-bearing), brilliant, anti-Apollo - and so beautiful because of it. But he has already cut off the chthonic umbilical cord (he does not have the force of life that is in the knotty stump of Fyodor Pavlovich) and walks like Agasfer, having got involved in the social-Caesar level, and here he is out of place and thin, not a fish in the water, unlike Pyotr Stepanovich Verkhovensky. And Svidrigailov is more smooth (not without reason something of the nobleman Jagaila can be heard in his surname and all his behavior in the novel is chivalrous), an armored lizard, obese, stinking and bloody, heavy, and he has no supply of moisture and the power of life, and that is why he is drawn to the dungeon of Hades (the spider in the other world), and he, hopelessly dry, surrounded by the outer St. Petersburg damp (the downpour-flood on the night of his suicide) in this ocean of primordial cosmic waters, sinks to the bottom: shoots himself and by fire returns himself to the Tartarus of the Titans. Chthonic male deities are conjugated, as titans, with Russian Gaea, the materio-raw earth. It is not for nothing that they are not Petersburgers, near-earthlings, from the universal space; and this is the village for Petersburg. They are landlords: Bykov, Svidrigailov; Fyodor Karamazov is a hardened provincial. In St. Petersburg, they are visitors, visitors. And Stavrogin is the first in the village: in a small town is his arena. In Rome, he will be the second - there Cæsar first ... In Stavrogin, despite all his Western gloss, can be heard irrepressible worthless power of the Russian ataman (he is the ataman of the party, its mystical, not practically-organizational head), which would be on the Volga and Siberia to spread out, not in the arena of parliamentary-political casemates player to make himself. And what does he care about petty women Lebyadkins or Elizabeths? He throws her overboard into the surging wave. And himself too.

This, chthonic layer of characters is a pole of Fire-Stone = Olympus, its social, creative-organizing civilizing Zeus' work. He is supersocial and transcendent. And the most meaningful incomprehensibility belongs to the heroes of this plan - they are sphinxes. And the sphinx is a lion-maiden: chthonic, like a woman, and at the same time sunny (a lion). In him, the clear and black sun have come together in one flesh. And these characters walk

---

[4] The name Fyodor is a contraction of Theodores - God's gift (Greek).

through the novel in the midst of moral and metaphysical problems that torment still human beings like Raskolnikov, Shatov or even Kirillov - like Chukovsky's Crocodile in the streets of Petrograd. For them there are no moral and metaphysical problems, for they themselves are the whole of metaphysics and united transcendence. In them there is a pre-spiritual state of the Whole, syncretic, before the disintegration into matter and spirit. Though they reason sometimes, but so, with their left foot, playfully, there are no problems for them; it is all a trifle in comparison with that Atlantean weight of being that they have to bear. Kronos is deeper than Zeus and more his witch doctor, for he only knows firelight, and this one smells the substance, mother and many other things, which are inexplicable by intellect and enlisted by him in the department of "irrational". And from the slime - life, like the healthy mud in Chernyshevsky's "What is to be done?" by Chernyshevsky (though rotten mud may be even more metaphysical and vital).

So, perhaps, Fyodor and Peter, Kron-Khton and Stone-Kesar[10] cannot oppose each other, for they belong to different levels, states of the Whole. Fyodor is conjugated to the aeon of the titans, and beneath him Chaos moves and pulsates its protoplasm. They, Peter and Fyodor, do not care about each other, they only squint at each other. And it is not without reason that Fyodor Dostoevsky gave his name, i.e. the name of God the Creator of the world of his heroes, to Father Karamazov, thus bringing him closer to the very center of the Psycho-Cosmo-Logos in his glorious way (the Church Slavonic prefixdosto-, like prepo-, means a superior degree of quality, the essence of prefixes for epithets of the deity). And that Stavrogin is the same level of being as Fyodor Pavlovich, who is Zosima in perspective, and in that plot turn comes out when he goes to confession to Tikhon, i.e. only this one can understand him, they have a common language, for they are of the same level. After all, even Ivan Karamazov in his conversation with Zosima is a child, a sucker, not on an equal level. And Stavrogin can be on an equal footing, because he does not just sin intellectually, like Ivan - he is dry and clean, so that for the full realization of this potency in Dostoevsky's Cosmos, it was necessary to irrigate him, to sprinkle him with Smerdyakov - but he sinned in a living way and touched being alive.

In the novel worlds, the chthonic layer, as a vitalization, as the first dark, moist sky of the primary cosmic waters, the sky of Varuna-Uranus, encircles the vastness of all the subsequent plots, characters, luminaries, airs and their relations = =relations, conflicts-affects, which, kesari and svetra, are all inside the first ones and are realized. In any case, this is the force field from which the waves, the pulsation of forces and impulses, the plant and the idea of all the plots in the novels: from Stavro-gin - the cataclysm of "The Devils", from Fyodor Pavlovich - the myrrh with which the Karamazov family is smeared both in composition and in dynamics: in it is the knot of all their passions, impulses and temptations. From Versilov is the Podrostok, and his whole world and plan is located inside Versilov's factory, predetermined by him. And Svidrigailov appears before Raskolnikov as a kind of pre-colonial marvel, to which this one, like geese to thunder, raises his head, where it comes to him: "But Svidrigailov is also a way out...". You bet! Into such depths and spaces, which the dry virgin Old Believer-deacon never dreamed of.

This is how Dostoevsky's Cosmos can be presented. But at the end of this work one sees that with this approach the whole moral and spiritual problematic has fallen somewhere - it does not grasp it, perhaps, just as in the sphere of Kant's theoretical reason, which touches only nature and necessity, freedom of will and ethics, personality and "I" remain inscrutable. And this is the obstacle for making ends meet in further thinking about and penetrating into the Whole of the Psycho-Cosmo-Logos, from which only the Cosmos is detached here. One can try to depict the hierarchy of roles in some scheme. If the Whole is Spheros, the levels in it can be seen as concentric spheres, each being binary, in a pair of opposites.

In the first scheme, the world is in the womb of the chthonic, like Jonah in the whale. And it is possible to see the world as an emanation from the pulsating interior, unfolding and dissolving. The human level is intermediate: it is spiraled (or stretched) on the one hand by chthonic-natural and raw mother earth (which is almost absent in Dostoevsky, zero), and on the other hand by spiritual-historical energies.

Time is mythical

In mythology, the "initial", "first" time, "right time", preceding empirical (historical) profane time. In V.m., primordial ancestors, demiurges, cultural heroes created the present state of the world and patterns and sanctions of social behavior. V. m. is the time of primordial creation, primordial objects and primordial actions; it is reflected first of all in cosmogonic, anthropogonic, etiological myths (cf., for example, the sphere of actions of the Raven and his family). For mythological thinking, V. m. appears to be the sphere of primary causes of subsequent real empirical actions; the explanation of the structure of a thing is identical to the story of how it was made; the description of the world around us is equal to the story of its creation. Mythical time is the primary source not only of causes, archetypal primordial images, but also of magical spiritual forces, which, being activated by rituals staging the events of V. m. (especially during calendar holidays, initiation, etc.), continue to maintain order in nature and society.

The magical emanation of the V. m. reaches the living bearers of the myth through rituals and dreams (cf. al'chera, "the time of dreams" in Aranda). The category of V. m. is especially characteristic of archaic mythologies, but transformed ideas about it are also found in developed mythologies, for example, as a golden age or as a zpoha of chaos, subject to ordering by the forces of the cosmos. Mythological initial times are used as a background in archaic epics ("The Old Elda", "Enuma Elish", etc.). In classical forms of epic, time similar to V. m. is also presented as initial, as the time of action of the ancestors who predetermined the subsequent order (cf. the era of King Arthur, the era of Yao and Shun, etc.).

The linear model of Mythical Time (the dichotomy "initial time/empirical time") was supplemented by the cyclic model of time, which was facilitated by the ritual repetition of the events of V. M., as well as calendar myths and the development of ideas about the dying and resurrecting god. Myths about the cyclic change of the chain of world epochs are connected with the cyclic model of time (cf., for example, the ideas about the change of yugas and kalpas). In eschatological myths there is also an image of end times, the death of the world, subject or not to cyclic renewal (cf., for example, Ragnarök, the doctrine of Mani, etc.).

Chthonic creatures

(from Greek chthonos - "earth"), mythological characters associated simultaneously with the productive power of the earth (water) and the killing potency of the underworld.

Actually Chthonic beings - born of the earth (cf. Greek Gaea, Russian Mother of the Raw Earth) or emerged from the earth, located in its depths (cf. Finnish Maakhis), retaining the features of Chthonic animals - snakes (see Nagi), amphibians, etc. (cf. Kekropa, half-snake - half-man, born by Gaea, Bague in Chib-Cha, Nommo in Dogon, etc.). (cf. Kekropa, a half-snake - a half-man born of Gaea, Bague in the Chibcha, Nommo in the Dogon, etc.), often have the appearance of monsters (cf. Tu-bo, etc.). The earth itself in a number of traditions was represented as a kind of H. s: vegetation - its wool, legs - peninsulas, etc. (cf. Myth yyz and Mow-nyamy).

Chthonic animals are associated with the depths of the earth, the roots of the world tree, the beginning of creation: Ahi Budhnya - the "serpent of the depths" in Vedic mythology, Hindu Shesha, Aido-Hvedo at the Phon, the turtle, on which the earth is held in various traditions (cf. The Khmer crocodile spirit Kron Pali, the Komi Yen and Omol'u, the Evenki Baha in the form of frogs-demiurges, the Kachin demiurge Mutum, who poured the earth on the fish swimming in the primordial ocean, and others. Characteristic are anthropogonic myths about the creation of people from the earth - the Chinese ancestress Nyuva, half-woman - half-snake, molds people from clay (cf. representations about autochthons, mythical original inhabitants of the earth, region, who went underground with the appearance of new population (Russian Chud, Sammodian Sikhirtya, Malagasy Wazimba).

Chthonic creatures are also associated with marriage symbolism: Nyuwa and Fushi in the form of dragons with intertwined tails; Targitai's marriage to the snake goddess (see Api) in Scythian mythology; the marriage of the hunter-hivaro to the water goddess Tsunghi, who turned into a snake; the motif of the frog princess, etc.

The marriage of a hero with a chthonic goddess meant possession of the land (country). Chthonic features have the image of a mother goddess, a mythical progenitor, associated also with death (chaos - cf. the Akkadian Tiamat), from the Australian Kunapipi to Demeter and Persephone; cf. the Aztec Tlasol'keotl'a (excrement-eating goddess), the Sumero-Akkadian Ereshkigal, and so on. The ambivalent character of chthonic deities is revealed by the motifs of marriage with the heavenly god who banished his wife to the lower world (cf. Numi-Torum and Kaltash-ekva among the Ob Ugrians, Yes and Hosedzm among the Kets, Pemba and Muso Koroni Kund'e among the Bambara). The dead living in the afterlife (underworld) - ancestors (see Lars, etc.) were referred to H. s..

The rivals of the demiurge, the lords of the underworld, also have a chthonic character (cf. Aztec. Tezcatlipok, the rival of Ketsal'koatl, Kul-otyr, the rival of Numi-Torum, etc.). The Greek cult of the chthonic deities - Hades, Persephone, Hecate - was mainly propitiatory in nature (cf. Ital. pa-liki, Ain. Toiekunra, etc.).

Conclusion

And regarding chthonics... We used that word to refer to all creatures that serve Melkor of their own free will. Orcs are warped, enslaved elves, they serve out of compulsion. Chthonics are the Maiar, the dragons, the Thuringwethili, the Karharoths.

Accordingly, for us chthonic is a collective designation of dark, pagan, infernal forces, primordial chaos

Chthonic twenty-four hours is a time or a kind of literary chronotope that allows the author to show parallel worlds at the same time.

Having researched literary works and delved into the lives of some literary creators using the sphere of chthonic time the following conclusions were drawn:

1.   Chthonic time helps to reveal the broader structure of literary images and to identify individual moments of the writers' work

2.   The chthonic day problem exists on a subconscious level and helps creative people along the way

3.   The ability to recognize chthonic imagery and trace chthonic time makes the reader a co-author of the work or a contemporary of the writer, allowing for a better understanding of literary information

This work can be used in literature lessons, elective classes, in psychological research, as well as for writing, in the future, scientific works

Literature

1. A.M. Stepanov "Big Dictionary of Esoteric Terms", M., 1971

2. F.M.Dostoevsky "White Nights" M., 1985.

3. F.M.Dostoevsky "Crime and Punishment" M., 1985

4. F.M. Dostoevsky "The Brothers Karamazov" M., 1979

5. A.S. Pushkin "Eugene Onegin" M., 1987

6. L.N. Tolstoy "War and Peace" M., 1981

7. M. Bulgakov "The Master and Margarita", M. 1998

8. N.V. Gogol "Viy" M., 1986.

9. N.V. Gogol "Evenings on a Farm near Dikanka" M., 1985

10. W Shakespeare's "Hamlet" M., 1997.

11. V.A.Zhukovsky "Svetlana" M., 1990.

12. C. Esenin "Black Man" M., 1989

13. I.V. Goethe's "The Forest King". M., 1978

14. G.D. Grachev "National Images of the World" M. 1988

15. Homer's "The Odyssey," "The Iliad."

appendix

49

 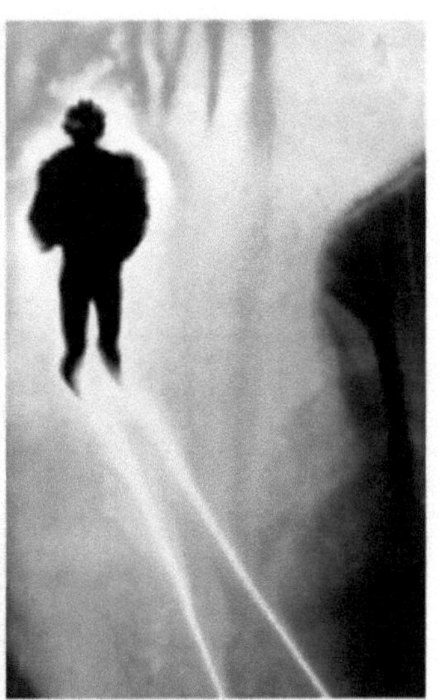

Principum amicitias!

Best
Dress

yes
I want morebooks!

Buy your books fast and straightforward online - at one of world's fastest growing online book stores! Environmentally sound due to Print-on-Demand technologies.

Buy your books online at
www.morebooks.shop

Kaufen Sie Ihre Bücher schnell und unkompliziert online – auf einer der am schnellsten wachsenden Buchhandelsplattformen weltweit! Dank Print-On-Demand umwelt- und ressourcenschonend produziert.

Bücher schneller online kaufen
www.morebooks.shop

Printed by Books on Demand GmbH, Norderstedt / Germany